FAITH
IN FRIENDSHIP

My Friend Is
Christian

by Ann Tatlock

PURPLE TOAD
PUBLISHING

My Friend Is Buddhist
My Friend Is Christian
My Friend Is Hindu
My Friend Is Jewish
My Friend Is Muslim

PUBLISHER'S NOTE: The data in this book has been researched in depth, and to the best of our knowledge is factual. Although every measure is taken to give an accurate account, Purple Toad Publishing makes no warranty of the accuracy of the information and is not liable for damages caused by inaccuracies.

NOTE: All Scripture verses are taken from the New Revised Standard Version, c. 1989 Division of the Christian Education of the National Council of the Churches of Christ in the United States of America.

Printing   1   2   3   4   5   6   7   8   9

Publisher's Cataloging-in-Publication Data
Tatlock, Ann.
   My friend is Christian / written by Ann Tatlock.
      p. cm.
Includes bibliographic references and index.
ISBN 9781624690945
1. Christian life—Miscellanea —Juvenile literature. 2. Theology, Doctrinal—Juvenile literature. I. Series: Faith in Friendship
 BR140 2015
 230
                                      2014937126

eBook ISBN: 9781624690952

Contents

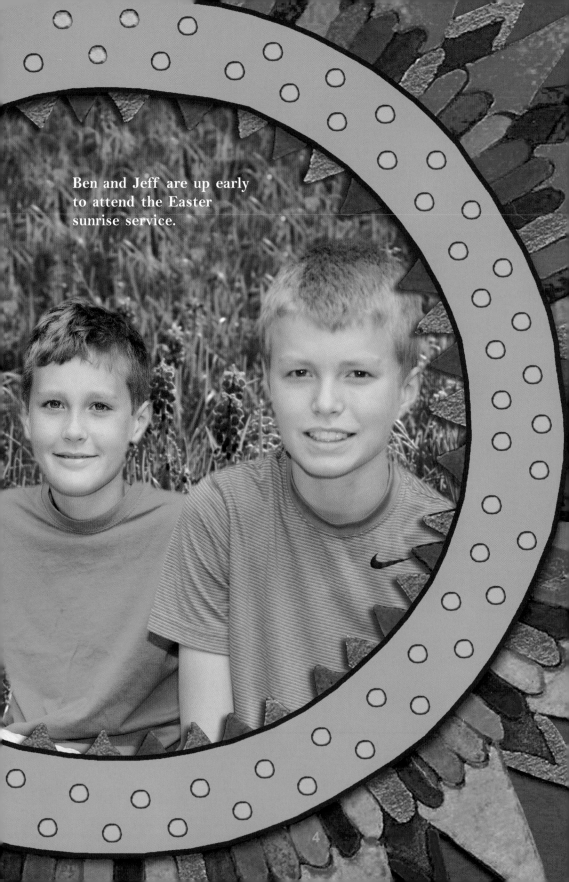

Ben and Jeff are up early
to attend the Easter
sunrise service.

4

Up Before the Sun: It's Easter Morning!

"Wake up, Ben," Mrs. Powell says. "You, too, Jeff. Time to get ready for the service."

Ben rolls over in the twin bed opposite mine. "Which service, Mom?" he asks. The room is still dark and he sounds grumpy.

Mrs. Powell laughs. "Don't you remember? Today is Easter Sunday. We're going to the sunrise service."

"Oh yeah!" Ben sits up and turns on the light. "Come on, Jeff. Let's get ready."

I hop out of bed. I've never been to an Easter service before, but my friend Ben invited me to go with his family this year. He said everyone is welcome to come sing songs and watch the sun come up, and afterward there's a big breakfast in the church basement. Then comes the best part of all—the Easter egg hunt. At age 10, Ben and I are getting a little old for the hunt. He says we can still get away with searching for the candy-filled eggs though, especially if we help his little sister fill her Easter basket.

When we arrive at the church, we join all the people who are already there, sitting on folding chairs set up in the grass.

"We don't always hold church outside, Jeff," Mr. Powell tells me. "We only do this on Easter morning. Usually we gather in the church sanctuary and worship there."

I smile and nod at Mr. Powell. He and my dad both work as executives at a large software company. My mom and Mrs. Powell have been friends since high school. Our families are a lot alike, except mine doesn't go to church.

Children hunt for colorful eggs on Easter morning. Eggs are a symbol of rebirth.

"I guess today is special," I say.

"It sure is," Mr. Powell says. "It's the most important day of the year."

I want to ask him why, but it's time for the service to start. For the next 45 minutes we sing and listen to the pastor talk and then we sing some more and watch the sun come up. It is not until our stomachs are full, our baskets filled with colorful eggs, and we're home again that I can ask Mr. Powell why Easter is so important.

"Why," he says, "Easter is the day Jesus rose from the dead." He smiles as he invites me and Ben to sit beside him on the couch.

"You mean, he died, but then he came back to life?" I ask.

"That's right," he explains. "It's called the Resurrection."

"But why did he die and why did he come back?"

"Well, let me tell you the story, Ben—"

"You mean, it's a story?"

Mr. Powell nods. "Yes. Christianity isn't just a set of beliefs or a set of rules and rituals. At the heart of Christianity is the story of God at work in the world. You and I and Ben—we're all a part of the story."

"Really?" I settle back to listen as Mr. Powell speaks.

***

The Resurrection of Christ by Raphael shows Jesus rising from the grave on the first Easter morning.

In the beginning, God created the heavens and the earth. He created the sun, the moon and the stars, the plants, the animals and the sea creatures. The best part of His creation, though, were men and women, whom He made in His own image.

People were meant to live in perfect relationship with God as well as with each other. But something happened that Christians call "The Fall." God gave people free will, which means they could choose to either obey or disobey Him. Sadly, after people were tempted by Satan, God's enemy, they chose to disobey.

As a result, the world became broken. Sin, suffering, sadness, and death all entered the world. The worst result was that the relationship between God and people was damaged. A holy God could no longer freely associate with people because they had become sinful.

But God continued to love the men, women, and children He had created. He called upon a certain group of people to be his chosen people, those through whom He would reveal His mercy and plan of salvation to the world. These were the Hebrews, who are also known as the Israelites or Jews. The Hebrew nation began when God called a man named Abraham to leave his homeland of Ur (present-day Iraq) and to settle in Canaan (present-day Israel).

From that one man came the mighty nation of Israel. In a world where most groups of people were polytheistic (believing in many gods), the Hebrews were monotheistic (believing in only one God), whom they knew as Yahweh. The name *Yahweh* is translated by most scholars as "I Am who I Am."

Through Hebrew priests, God explained how people's sins could be forgiven and they could be in a right relationship with Him. This was the sacrificial system, in which animals like doves or lambs were slain, with the blood symbolically covering the sins of the people. This seems harsh to us today, but it begins to make sense when we consider the perfect holiness of God.

The problem with the priestly sacrificial system was that each sacrifice granted only temporary pardons. The priests were constantly having to offer sacrifices because people continually chose to disobey.

But thankfully the Hebrew Scriptures (also known as the Old Testament) were full of prophecies concerning a coming Messiah who would deliver people from sin once and for all. God knew that when the time was right, He would send His own Son into the world to become "the Lamb of God, who takes away the sin of the world" (John 1:29).

You may wonder how it is that God had a Son. It's part of the mystery known as the Trinity. Christians believe there is only one God, but that He has three parts: Father, Son, and Holy Spirit. Sometimes these are called the Godhead. The Father, Son, and Holy Spirit are all equally part of the Godhead though they have different roles.

The Father sent the Son to enter the world to be its Savior. When Jesus was conceived in the womb of his mother Mary, it was no ordinary

In Da Vinci's *Annunciazione*, the angel Gabriel greets Mary with the news that she has been chosen to bear the Son of God.

conception. We know from the famous Christmas story in Luke 1 that the angel Gabriel appeared to Mary to tell her she would be the mother of the long-awaited Christ-child. Gabriel's appearance is called the Annunciation.

Gabriel told Mary she would conceive by the power of the Holy Spirit so that when Jesus was born he would be both fully human and fully God. There was no earthly father involved in the conception, although Joseph, to whom Mary was engaged, later became Jesus's father on Earth. On the day Jesus was born, Mary, Joseph, and a few lowly shepherds from nearby witnessed a great miracle known as the Incarnation. That is, God became part of His own creation in the form of a newborn baby.

The world Jesus entered was the ancient land of Israel. At that time, Israel was ruled by the powerful Roman Empire. The Romans were the enemies of the Jews, who longed to be free to rule themselves.

Jesus grew up in a Jewish home and followed Jewish customs. He studied the ancient Hebrew Scriptures and worshiped at a synagogue. At

Jesus spent three years preaching and teaching throughout Israel. Artist Henrik Olrik shows Jesus delivering one famous speech, the Sermon on the Mount.

the age of 30, he started his ministry of teaching and healing. He traveled from place to place with a core group of followers, the Twelve Disciples. Jesus performed many miracles, such as making the lame walk and the blind see. But more importantly, he told people how to find peace with God.

After three years of ministry, Jesus was crucified by the Romans. He was beaten with a whip and nailed to a cross. While he was dying, the Romans taunted him, saying, "If you're God, save yourself." He was God and he could have saved himself, but he chose to save humankind instead. Jesus chose to be the final sacrifice for the sins of humanity, so that people could come into God's holy presence.

After Jesus was pronounced dead, his followers took his body, laid it in a tomb that was like a cave, and sealed it with a large stone. On the third day after his death, they went to anoint his body with spices, but found the stone rolled away from the entrance and the tomb empty. Jesus's body wasn't there. God had raised him from the dead! Today, almost 2,000 years later, Christians still celebrate the Resurrection on Easter Sunday.

What Christians Believe in 111 Words

Early Christians found it necessary to put together a statement of faith, since some who called themselves followers of Christ were teaching doctrine contrary to what Jesus taught. For example, a Roman Christian named Marcion said that Jesus wasn't the Messiah proclaimed by the prophets and that the Old Testament wasn't divine scripture. By 180 CE, Roman Christians had developed an early form of what was called *The Apostles' Creed* to refute such heresy, or wrong teaching. Over the centuries, additions and revisions were made until finally, by the 8th century, The Apostles' Creed reached its present form. It sums up the doctrinal beliefs held by those in the various Christian denominations around the world.

The Apostles' Creed

I believe in God, the Father Almighty,
Creator of heaven and earth;
And in Jesus Christ, His only Son, our Lord;
Who was conceived by the Holy Spirit,
Born of the Virgin Mary,
Suffered under Pontius Pilate,
Was crucified, died, and was buried.
He descended into hell;
The third day he rose again from the dead;
He ascended into Heaven,
And is seated at the right hand of God, the Father Almighty;

The 12 apostles

From thence he shall come to judge the living and the dead.
I believe in the Holy Spirit,
The Holy Catholic Church,*
The Communion of Saints,
The forgiveness of sins,
The resurrection of the body,
And life everlasting. Amen.

*the true Christian church of all times and all places (not necessarily today's Catholic Church)

Three women, all named Mary, rejoice to see the resurrected Christ.

Traveling Through Time: Back to the Beginning

"If Jesus rose from the dead," I ask, "then where is he now?"

Mr. Powell smiles at me. "Well, Jeff, the Bible tells us that after Jesus appeared to his disciples and many other people to assure them he was alive, the Lord God took him to Heaven. This is called the Ascension. Jesus is now in Heaven, seated at the right hand of the Father, watching over us and even interceding for us, which means he prays for us."

"So when Jesus went to Heaven, did people start going to church like we did today?"

"No, not exactly. For a long time, there weren't any church buildings, and in fact, the earliest Christians didn't even call themselves Christians. They were Jewish and continued to think of themselves as Jewish. What set the first Christians apart from other Jews was that they believed Jesus was the promised Messiah. While Jesus didn't deliver them from the Romans, he did

The Apostle Paul as depicted by Pete Paul Rubens

something greater—he delivered them from sin and death. The early Christians saw Jesus conquer death by rising again."

"So when did people start going to church, Mr. Powell?"

"Well, Jeff, let me tell you the story of the church from the beginning."

***

The first church leaders were the Twelve Disciples, the men who had been with Jesus during the three years of his ministry. After the Resurrection, they became known as apostles. This group included Peter, James, and John, all of whom later wrote letters that became part of the New Testament.

The early church was centered in Jerusalem. On the first *Pentecost* after Jesus's resurrection, about 120 believers met together to pray and seek God's guidance. Pentecost is the Greek name of the Festival of Weeks, which was a prominent Jewish holiday. As these believers prayed, they felt the Holy Spirit come upon them, giving them power and wisdom to begin to spread the message of Jesus Christ. Some Christians describe Pentecost as the "birthday of the church."

Shortly afterward, Peter gave the first Christian sermon, which is recorded in the Bible in Acts 2. After hearing this sermon, about 3,000 people believed and were baptized. So began the growth of the church that continues to this day.

As the church grew, it became apparent that it needed leadership. A man named Stephen became the first deacon as well as the first Christian martyr, as he was condemned to death for preaching about Jesus. After that, many believers fled Jerusalem because of persecution. This dispersion only led to the spread of Christianity to other places because the church gained converts wherever the disciples went.[1]

In this 17th -century painting by Caravaggio, Paul falls from his horse on the road to Damascus after he encounters Jesus and is blinded by a flash of light.

One man who witnessed the death of Stephen was a Jewish Pharisee named Saul. He was himself one of the most zealous persecutors of the new believers. He viewed them as men and women who had fallen into heresy, and so he had many of them arrested, imprisoned, and executed.

Saul was on his way to Damascus in search of believers to arrest when he was struck down by a blinding light. As he fell to his knees he heard a voice say, "Saul, Saul, why do you persecute me?" Saul asked who was speaking and the voice said, "I am Jesus, whom you are persecuting. But get up and enter the city, and you will be told what you are to do" (Acts 9:5-6).

Blinded, Saul did what he was told. While in Damascus, a believer named Ananias prayed for him and baptized him. Saul's eyes were opened again and he became a believer. Not only that but Saul, whose name was changed to Paul, became one of the greatest Christian missionaries in history.

Paul spent the rest of his life traveling throughout the known world preaching salvation through Jesus Christ. He made it clear that Jesus came to save not only Jews but all people everywhere. As he wrote in his letter to the Romans, "Everyone who calls on the name of the Lord shall be saved" (Romans 10:13).

Thirteen of the letters Paul wrote to fellow believers and to the developing church became part of the New Testament. These are known as the Pauline Epistles. According to Christian tradition, Paul was arrested and martyred in Rome sometime in the mid-60s, during the reign of Nero.

Neither the Jews nor the Christians fared well under the Roman Empire. In the year 70, the Romans destroyed the city of Jerusalem and the Jewish temple. As for Christians, because they refused to worship the emperor, many were killed.

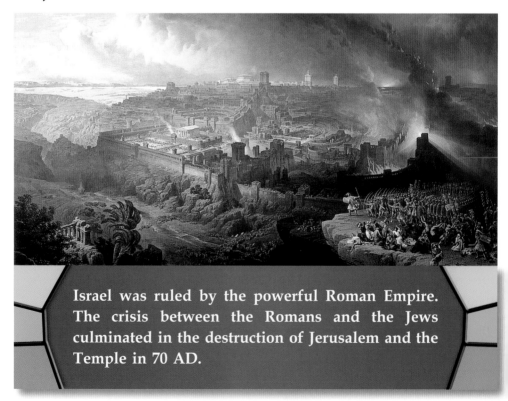

Israel was ruled by the powerful Roman Empire. The crisis between the Romans and the Jews culminated in the destruction of Jerusalem and the Temple in 70 AD.

Roman Emperor Constantine was the first to befriend the Christian church. His Edict of Milan paved the way for Christianity to become the official religion of the Roman Empire.

All this changed when Constantine became the Roman emperor. In 313, he issued the Edict of Milan, legalizing Christianity. For the first time, believers began to meet in church buildings rather than in private homes. Constantine gave gifts and property to the church and financed the copying of the Bible.

By the end of the 4th century, Christianity had become the official religion of the Roman Empire. To this day, the leader of the Catholic Church, the Pope, resides in Rome.

In 476, the fall of Rome signaled the beginning of the Middle Ages. By then, the church was well-established and had a great influence upon culture, especially in the West. Church buildings and cathedrals were erected, an intricate hierarchy of church leadership was formed, the Pope held power over kings, Catholic missionaries were sent around the globe, and the church presided over the events of believers' lives from birth to death.

For nearly ten centuries, Christians were unified. But in 1054 a schism arose. The church split into two factions, Roman Catholic and Eastern Orthodox. The latter is officially called the Orthodox Catholic Church.

Almost 500 years later, another change came to the church. A German priest named Martin Luther was troubled by some of the church's practices, especially the sale of indulgences. Professional "pardoners" sold these documents to people who wanted to shorten their time in purgatory, a middle ground between Earth and Heaven where souls are purified from sin.

Luther believed that salvation was gained by grace alone and wasn't aided by the sale of indulgences. For this and other practices that he considered corrupt, Luther called for reform. It was not his intention to leave the Catholic Church, but his excommunication was the beginning of the Protestant Reformation.

Martin Luther (1483–1546) was a Catholic priest whose attempts to reform the church resulted in the Protestant Reformation.

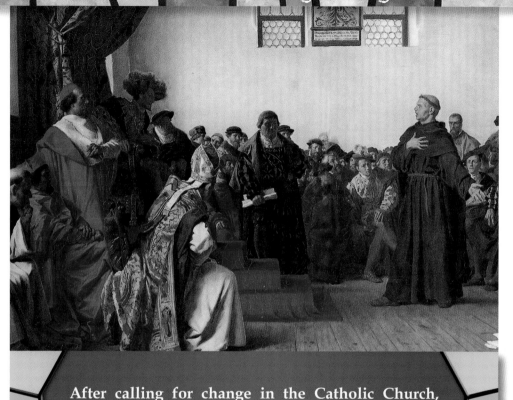

After calling for change in the Catholic Church, Martin Luther defended his convictions at court in the city of Worms, Germany.

Martin Luther was the founder of today's Lutheran Church. But since the time of the Reformation, many Protestant denominations have arisen, including Baptist, Methodist, Presbyterian, and Pentecostal.

The Protestant denominations and the Catholic Church today have unique practices and varying worship styles. They also maintain varying interpretations of certain Scriptures. But the one thing all Christians have in common is the conviction that Jesus is the Son of God and Savior of all who believe.

Catholics and Protestants: A Brief Comparison

Catholics and Protestants both read the Bible, pray, assemble to worship and sing hymns, and celebrate many of the same holy days. However, they have their differences too.[2]

Services
Catholic – Called Mass, the most important service is held on Sunday morning. Mass is also offered every day of the week.

Protestant – Generally called a Worship Service, these are held on Sunday mornings, although some denominations hold services on Wednesday nights as well.

Baptisms
Catholic – Practice infant baptism by sprinkling holy water on the forehead.

Protestant – Most Protestant denominations practice infant baptism, though others, like Baptists, believe a person must be old enough to understand the sacrament before being baptized. Baptists practice full body immersion rather than sprinkling.

Sign of the Cross
Catholic – Catholics perform the Sign of the Cross while praying, "In the name of the Father, and of the Son, and of the Holy Spirit. Amen." This is sometimes done while genuflecting, or bending one knee to the floor in worship.

Protestant – Most Protestant denominations do not perform the Sign of the Cross.

Pope

Catholic – The Pope is the "Vicar of Christ" and the visible head of the church on Earth.

Protestant – The Pope is the head of the Catholic Church, but does not have the authority to speak for the church as a whole.

Eucharist/Communion

Catholic – The bread and wine of the Eucharist become the actual body and blood of Christ when consecrated by the priest. This process is called Transubstantiation.

Protestant – The bread and the wine of Communion are symbols only and a commemoration of Christ's death.

Confession

Catholic – Catholics make confession to and receive absolution from a priest.

Protestant – Believers confess their sins directly to God through prayer.

Purgatory

Catholic – Catholics believe Purgatory is a middle ground after death where souls are cleansed in preparation for Heaven.

Protestant – Protestants believe the soul upon death is immediately in the presence of God.

Christians view the beauty of nature as the handiwork of a loving Creator God.

The Bible: God Talking to Us

Everything Mr. Powell has told me makes me wonder about something. "Since God is invisible," I ask, "how do you know so much about Him?"

"Good question, Jeff," Mr. Powell says. "Ben and I have talked about that too. Remember, Ben?"

Ben nods. "Sure. It's because He told us, right?"

Mr. Powell laughs. "Yes, but I think Jeff means, how did He tell us? And that has to do with something we call revelation."

"Revelation? What's that?"

"Well, Jeff, let me tell you."

***

Christians believe God has made known both His being and His character through general and special revelation. General revelation refers to the ways in which the existence of God is shown through his creation. Psalm 19:1 says, "The heavens are telling the glory of God; and the firmament proclaims his handiwork." We see Him through the beauty in the world, but also in the mere fact that the world exists in such a way as to support human life. Everything our bodies need—air to breathe, water to drink, food to eat—is provided by the earth. Christians reason that such a complex and intricate design points to a Designer.[1]

Even so, creation doesn't tell us the specifics about God. This is where special revelation comes in. God told us everything we need to know about Himself through two important means. One is through Jesus Christ. As already explained, Christians consider Jesus to be God in the flesh.

The second important means of revelation is the Bible, the book that Christians consider the inspired Word of God. The Bible isn't just one book, however. It is actually 66 books written by some 40 authors on three continents over approximately 1,600 years.[2] And yet these books present a unified picture of God working in the world without contradicting each other.

The Bible is divided into two parts, the Old Testament (OT), which was written in Hebrew and Aramaic, and the New Testament (NT), written in Greek. The 39 books of the OT include history, prophecy, law, wisdom, and poetry. Moses recorded the first five books of the OT, or the Pentateuch, around 1440 BCE. The last book of the OT is Malachi, which was written in 460 BCE.

Nothing more was added to the Bible until the four Gospels were written to record the life and ministry of Jesus. These are the books that begin the New Testament. The earliest of these, the Gospel of Mark, was determined by scholars to have been written between 55 and 65 CE. Mark was not a disciple of Jesus but a missionary who accompanied Paul on his first missionary journey.

Two of the Gospels were written by disciples of Jesus. They are eyewitness accounts of his life, teachings, and resurrection. These are the Gospels of Matthew and John.

The fourth Gospel was written by a physician named Luke. He was a close companion of Paul and other leaders of the early church. He also

Though not among the original disciples of Jesus, Luke later became a believer and a leader in the early church.

wrote the book of Acts, which records the formation of the early church. Luke is the only known Gentile (non-Jewish) author of the NT.

Most of the remaining books of the NT are letters that Christian leaders, including Paul, Peter, James, John, and Jude, wrote to various churches or individuals. These offer spiritual truths and practical advice for Christian living.

The final book of the NT is Revelation. It was written by the Apostle John around 95 CE. John, one of Christ's original disciples, was living in exile on the Isle of Patmos when he wrote Revelation. He wrote it to give hope to Christians who were suffering severe persecution for their faith. He also wrote it to tell people what God was planning to do at the end of time. Christians believe that many of the events spoken of in Revelation are yet to come.

The Apostle John was one of the first chosen by Jesus to be a disciple. Besides the Gospel of John and Revelation, John wrote three letters that are also included in the NT.

While the books of the NT were written relatively close in time, the Bible as we know it today didn't come together all at once. Over several centuries, many books were written that claimed to speak authoritatively on Christian history and doctrine. Finally, church leaders realized they needed to identify which ones were true revelations of God and which were simply the opinions of people.

While Christians concede that all the books of the Bible were written by human hands, they believe at the same time the minds of those men were inspired by the Holy Spirit. The word *inspired* means "God-breathed." In other words, God guided these human writers according to His will.

Beginning in 325 CE, church leaders met in councils to decide which books should be added to the 39 books of the OT. The process of canonization—that is, choosing the books inspired by God—took several decades. Finally, the 27 books that now comprise the NT were settled upon and the Bible was completed.[3]

The Catholic Bible differs from the Protestant Bible in that it includes the Apocrypha. This is a group of books written during the 400 years between the writing of the last OT book and the first NT book. As such, they're placed together between the testaments.

The books of the Bible were copied by hand for hundreds of years before the invention of the printing press. This tedious and detailed work was often done by monks. The *scriptorium* was a special room in a monastery where monks would spend many hours with quill pens and parchment, copying the Scriptures without candlelight or heat. This was done to keep the parchment from catching fire.

The work of these scribes has been found to be remarkably accurate. One way scholars test the historical accuracy of ancient manuscripts is to

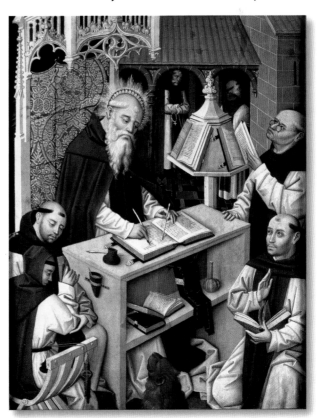

St. Jerome and his fellow monks laboriously copied the books of the Bible by hand.

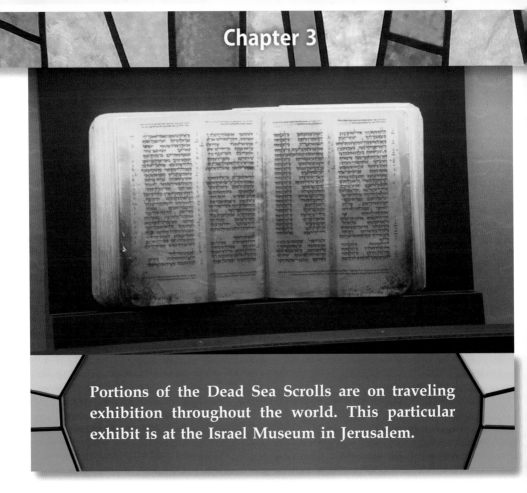

Portions of the Dead Sea Scrolls are on traveling exhibition throughout the world. This particular exhibit is at the Israel Museum in Jerusalem.

look at the agreement between the earliest copies and the last copies made before the printing press. In testing the books of the Bible, scholars have found human error, but all errors had to do with small details like numbers, names, and places. No errors were detected that involve the central beliefs of Christianity.[4]

In 1947, an amazing discovery was made near the Dead Sea in Israel. A shepherd boy wandered into a cave and discovered nearly 500 scrolls, about 100 of which were copies of the OT. These included fragments of every OT book except Esther.

From that time until 1956, a total of 11 caves were discovered where scrolls had been stored by an ancient Jewish community known as the Essenes. Many of the scrolls were stored in pottery jars that helped to preserve them for 2,000 years. Among the findings was a complete manuscript for the OT book of Isaiah.[5] The Dead Sea Scrolls have been an important aid in studying the authenticity and integrity of today's Bible.

Talking to God

For Christians, Bible reading and prayer go hand in hand. Reading the Bible is listening to God talk to His followers, while prayer is talking with God.

Many ritual prayers are centuries old and are recited either daily or on special occasions. Some prayers are unique to Catholics and others to Protestants, but one prayer that both branches of Christianity have in common is The Lord's Prayer. This is the prayer Jesus taught his disciples to pray.

The Lord's Prayer
Our Father, who art in heaven,
Hallowed be thy Name.
Thy Kingdom come.
Thy will be done on earth,
As it is in heaven.
Give us this day our daily bread.
And forgive us our trespasses,
As we forgive those who trespass against us.
And lead us not into temptation,
But deliver us from evil.
For Thine is the kingdom,
The power, and the glory,
Forever.
Amen.

From Christ's example, each Christian understands that prayer should include praise and thanksgiving, confession, supplication, and intercession.

Christians give praise to God for who He is and thanksgiving for what He has done. We confess our sins so He can forgive us, while at the same time we forgive those who have hurt us. Supplication is asking God to meet our daily needs, and intercession is praying for the needs of others.

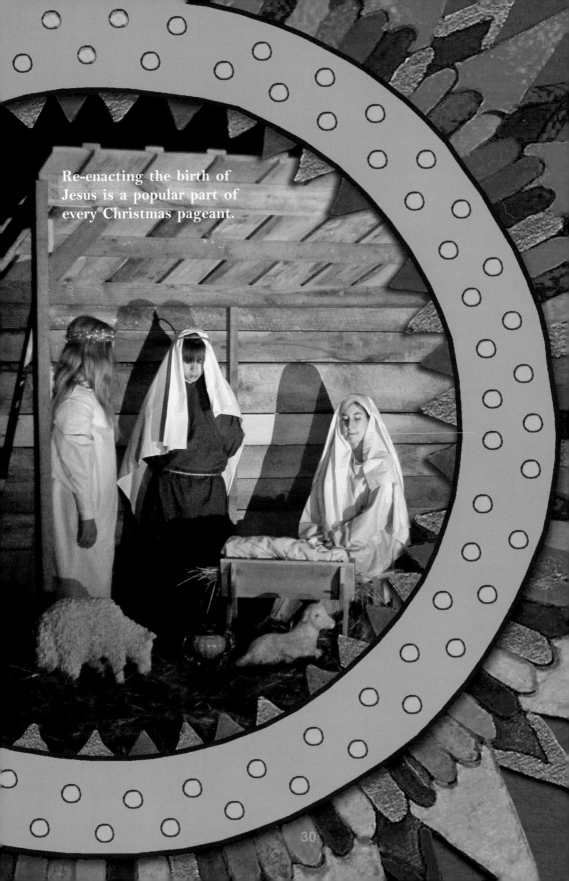

Re-enacting the birth of Jesus is a popular part of every Christmas pageant.

Holy Days in the Christian Calendar

"I wish I could be like that shepherd boy and find something like those scrolls in a cave." I look at Ben to see what he thinks.

"Yeah, me too!" he says. "And guess what . . . when part of the Dead Sea Scrolls were on display in a museum, we got to go see them."

"Cool! Could you understand what they said?"

"No way!" Ben laughs. "They were written in Hebrew. I don't read Hebrew."

Mr. Powell says, "That's why it's so important that the Bible has been translated into over 2,000 languages. That way, people around the world can read it for themselves."

"So people around the world celebrated Easter like we did today, Mr. Powell?"

"Oh, yes. Christians everywhere celebrate important holy days. You'd recognize these

Christian holidays because they've become part of our Western culture and are celebrated in various ways even by non-Christians."

"Do you mean, like Christmas?"

"Yes, like Christmas. And since that's when Christ was born into the world, that's a good place to start."

***

The Christian year starts with the first Sunday in Advent, the four-week period before Christmas. The word *advent* comes from Latin and means "to come." Advent is a time to spiritually prepare for the coming of Christ.

One of the most popular practices of Advent is lighting the candles on the Advent wreath. The wreath is made of evergreen branches that symbolize God's promise of eternal life. The trimmings are placed in a circle on a table, with four candles placed among the branches. In the center is a taller candle called the Christ candle.

One candle is lit on the first Sunday of Advent, two are lit on the second Sunday and so forth until finally all four candles and the Christ candle are lit on Christmas day. Scripture reading, prayers, and hymn singing accompany the lighting of the candles.[1]

The earliest Christians, in keeping with Old Testament feasts and festivals, designated the day of Christ's birth as the Feast of the Nativity. The celebration began with a special mass called "Christ's Mass," which later simply became known as Christmas.[2]

No one knows exactly when Jesus was born, but the day chosen to celebrate his birthday is December 25th. The first recorded instance of it being celebrated on this day was in 336 CE, when Constantine was the emperor of Rome. A few years later, Pope Julius I declared December 25th the official date of Christmas.[3]

The Christmas season is a time of great festivity. In the days leading up to and including December 25th, homes are decorated with colorful electric lights, wreaths, and candles. Christmas trees are trimmed with ornaments, and stockings are hung by the fireplace. Cards and gifts are exchanged between families, friends, and coworkers. Kitchens are filled with baked goods and hot spiced apple cider, folks go caroling through neighborhoods, and churches hold special Christmas Eve services.

Christians often display nativity scenes in their homes or on their lawns. These scenes re-create the story of Christ's birth as portrayed in the Gospels of Luke and Matthew.

Because of a Roman census, Mary and Joseph were required to travel to Bethlehem just as Mary was due to deliver her baby. The couple tried to find lodging at an inn but there were no rooms left. The innkeeper allowed Mary and Joseph to spend the night in his barn. In that lowly, rustic place, God's Son entered the world. His first cradle was a manger, an open box that held food for cattle.

Luke chapter 2 tells about three shepherds who were watching their flocks nearby when they were visited by an angel. The angel told them not to be afraid because he brought them the good news that the Messiah had been born. The angel told the shepherds where to find him.

On the night of the nativity, an angel appeared to three shepherds to tell them the Savior had been born in Bethlehem. A bright star guided them to the city.

Matthew chapter 2 tells about the three wise men from the East who followed the Star of Bethlehem to the birthplace of Jesus, bringing him gifts of gold, frankincense, and myrrh. Included in today's nativity scenes, along with Jesus, Mary, and Joseph, are the shepherds and wise men who visited Jesus when he was born.

As wonderful a holiday as Christmas is, Easter is of even greater importance to Christians because it commemorates the death and resurrection of Christ. The days and weeks leading up to Easter Sunday are also marked by ritual celebrations, beginning with Ash Wednesday.

Ash Wednesday is 46 days before Easter. The date of Easter varies because it is calculated according to the lunar months, just like the Jewish festival of Passover on which it is based. Lunar months do not coincide with calendar months.[4]

During Ash Wednesday services, ashes are used to draw a cross on the forehead of worshipers as a symbol of repentance and a reminder of human mortality.

Ash Wednesday opens the season of Lent, which commemorates the 40 days Jesus spent fasting in the wilderness between the time of his baptism and his ministry. Lent is meant to be a time of prayer and fasting for believers.

Ash Wednesday

The final week of Lent is Holy Week, the high point of the church's calendar. The first day of Holy Week is Palm Sunday, which marks Jesus's entry into Jerusalem for the start of Passover. Because the biblical account tells of people welcoming Jesus with palm branches, many churches today use palm branches during their services.

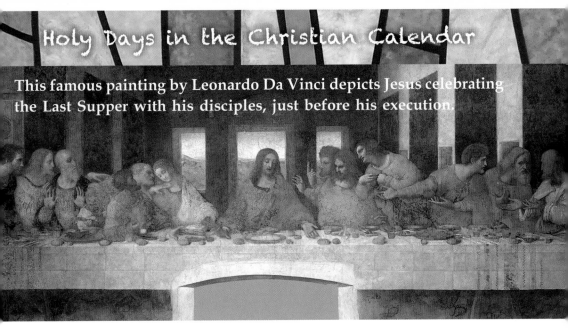

This famous painting by Leonardo Da Vinci depicts Jesus celebrating the Last Supper with his disciples, just before his execution.

Palm Sunday is followed by Maundy Thursday, the day on which Jesus is said to have held the Last Supper with his disciples. Knowing he would be crucified by the Romans the next day, Jesus offered his followers bread and wine to symbolize his body and blood, which would be given for their salvation. Today, the ritual that recalls this event is called the Eucharist (Catholic) or Communion (Protestant).

The Friday of Holy Week is called Good Friday and is the day Christians remember Christ's death on the cross. It may seem strange to call a day good when it was the day someone died, but Christians use the term because of what Christ's death accomplished.

The Bible records a symbolic event that coincided with Christ's death. A thick curtain hung in the Jewish temple that separated the Holy of Holies from the rest of the temple. The Holy of Holies was considered God's dwelling place. No one could enter except for the high priest, and that happened only once a year. At the moment Jesus died, the curtain in the temple was torn from top to bottom, symbolizing that a way had been made for people to step into the presence of God.

Holy Week culminates in the joyous celebration of Easter, discussed in Chapter One. Of course, there are other Holy Days in the Christian calendar, especially for Catholics who celebrate many Saints' days. But Christmas, Easter, and the days surrounding them are the highlights of the Christian year, as believers remember the birth, death, and resurrection of Jesus Christ.

Santa Claus and the Easter Bunny

Whether Christian or not, everyone recognizes two traditional, Christian holiday figures: Santa Claus and the Easter Bunny. But where did they come from exactly?

Santa Claus is based on a real person, a man named Saint Nicholas who lived in Myra (a town in modern-day Turkey) in the 4th century. He was a wealthy man who had a tender heart for the poor and a special love for children. While still a young man, Nicholas became the Bishop of Myra and spent his life helping those in need.

The most famous story about Saint Nicholas has to do with a wealthy shipping merchant who lost all his ships and cargo during a storm. The loss left the man poor. He had three daughters of marrying age but was unable to provide them with dowries required for marriage. Nicholas grieved for the man and wondered what would become of him and his daughters.

Nicholas wanted to help but he knew the man wouldn't want to take charity. So one night he decided to drop a bag of gold coins through an open window in the eldest daughter's room. Some of those coins fell into a stocking that had been hung out to dry. From this story, it's easy to see where the idea of a mysterious visitor leaving gifts came from!

Through the centuries and across continents Saint Nicholas became known by many names, including Father

St. Nicholas and the
"Oschter Haws"

Christmas and Kris Kringle. Eventually the Dutch name "Sinterklaas" became the modern English translation of Santa Claus.[5]

Although the origins of the Easter bunny are unclear, the legend of this egg-laying rabbit may have come to America in the 18th century when German immigrants brought with them the story of "Osterhase" or "Oschter Haws." This bunny gave gifts of colored eggs to good children who made nests of their caps and bonnets before Easter. These nests later became baskets and candy was added along with eggs.[6]

Although the Easter bunny and colored eggs both have their symbolic roots in pagan religions, Christianity adopted them and gave them new meaning. The rabbit, a symbol of fertility, represents rebirth and new life. The egg, also an ancient symbol of new life, represents for Christians the resurrection of Jesus from the tomb.

Mass is celebrated in a Catholic Church in Basoko, Democratic Republic of the Congo.

A Final Thought

Since the first handful of rough-hewn men and women walked with Jesus two thousand years ago, Christianity has grown to become one of the major religions of the world.

By the year 2010, a comprehensive study showed that 2.18 billion people around the world identified themselves as Christians. That's roughly one-third of the Earth's population.[1] This number includes people of all ages, races, and cultures.

Today, Christianity continues to grow, especially in Asia, Africa, and Latin America. China alone is home to an estimated 90 million Christians, and on the continent of Africa there are approximately 400 million believers. It's estimated that by 2025, two-thirds of the world's Christians will live in Africa, Latin America, and Asia.[2]

St. Peter's Basilica, in Vatican City, is the center of Roman Catholicism. It is built on the site where St. Peter died a martyr and where he was buried in 64 CE. St. Peter is considered the first pope, and Vatican City is where the present pope still resides.

The Apostle Peter is one who walked with Jesus when he was alive. Peter went on to start the church after Jesus's Resurrection and Ascension. The book of Acts records what Peter discovered about God as he went about preaching the Gospel: "I truly understand that God shows no partiality, but in every nation anyone who fears him and does what is right is acceptable to him" (Acts 10:34).

That means God loves everyone in the world equally, no matter what the person's background is or what they have done in life.

Jesus shows both his power and compassion by healing a man who had been paralyzed for 38 years.

BCE

2000 The Hebrew nation of Israel is formed, beginning with Abraham. It is prophesied that the Savior of the world will arise from there.

4 BCE—1CE Jesus is born in Bethlehem, Israel. (Scholars are not sure exactly when he was born, but they estimate it was between 4 BCE and 1 CE.) Eventually, the calendar will be reset to his birth.

CE

26 Jesus begins his ministry along with his Twelve Disciples.

33 Jesus is crucified and then resurrected. The Christian church is established under the leadership of the apostles.

35 Saint Paul is converted.

48 Paul begins his missionary journeys, during which time he writes many of the letters that later are included in the New Testament.

60-100 The four gospel accounts of the life of Jesus (Matthew, Mark, Luke, and John) are written.

66-70 The Jews revolt against Rome; Jerusalem is destroyed in 70.

313 Constantine, the emperor of Rome, issues the Edict of Milan, legalizing Christianity.

380 Christianity is recognized as the official religion of the Roman Empire.

476 Rome falls. The Middle Ages begin.

1054 The Church splits, creating the Roman Catholic Church and the Eastern Orthodox Church.

1517 Martin Luther initiates what will become known as the Protestant Reformation. The Church splits again, with Protestants breaking away from Catholicism. Numerous Protestant denominations are formed in the years to come.

1947 The Dead Sea Scrolls are discovered.

2010 The number of Christians around the world reaches 2.18 billion.

2013 Cardinal Jorge Mario Bergoglio of Buenos Aires, Argentina, becomes the 266th pope of the Roman Catholic Church. He is known as Pope Francis.

Chapter 2 Traveling Through Time: Back to the Beginning

1. Michael Collins and Matthew A. Price. *The Story of Christianity* (New York: DK Publishing, Inc., 1999), p. 30.
2. "Comparison Between Orthodoxy, Protestantism & Roman Catholicism," *Christianity in View,* accessed on April 23, 2013, http://christianityinview.com/comparison.html

Chapter 3 The Bible: God Talking to Us

1. James Stuart Bell with Sam O'Neal, *The Bible Answer Book* (Naperville, IL: Sourcebooks, Inc., 2010), p. 14.
2. "What Is the Bible?" *Christian Apologetics and Research Ministry,* accessed on April 23, 2013, www.carm.org/what-bible
3. Bell, p. 15.
4. Ibid, pp. 20-22.
5. Michael Collins and Matthew A. Price, *The Story of Christianity* (New York: DK Publishing, Inc., 1999) p. 19.

Chapter 4 Holy Days in the Christian Calendar

1. Martha Zimmerman, *Celebrating the Christian Year* (Minneapolis: Bethany House Publishers, 1993), p. 33.
2. Ibid, p. 24.
3. "Why is Christmas Day on the 25th of December?" *Why Christmas?,* accessed on April 30, 2013, www.whychristmas.com
4. Jonathan Hill, *What Has Christianity Ever Done for Us?* (Downers Grove, IL: Intervarsity Press, 2005), p. 20.
5. Zimmerman, pp. 51-54.
6. "Where Did the Easter Bunny Come From?" *The Christian Post,* accessed May 3, 2013, http://www.christianpost.com/news/where-did-the-easter-bunny-come-from-92695/

Chapter 5 A Final Thought

1. "Global Christianity: A Report on the Size and Distribution of the World's Christian Population," *The Pew Forum,* accessed on May 15, 2013, http://www.pewforum.org/2011/12/19/global-christianity-exec/
2. Ron Benrey, *The Complete Idiot's Guide to Christian Mysteries* (New York: Penguin Group, 2008), pp. 244-245.

Books

DK Illustrated Family Bible. New York: DK Publishing, 2013.

Graham, Ruth Bell. One Wintry Night. Nashville: Thomas Nelson, Inc., 1994, 2012.

Hale, Rosemary Drage. Understanding Religions: Christianity. New York: The Rosen Publishing Group, Inc., 2010.

Ham, Ken, and Bodie Hodge. Begin: A Journey Through Scriptures for Seekers and New Believers. Green Forest, AR: Master Books, 2011.

Hanegraaff, Hank. The Creation Answer Book. Nashville: Thomas Nelson, Inc., 2012.

Works Consulted

Bell, James Stuart, with Sam O'Neal. The Bible Answer Book. Naperville, IL: Sourcebooks, Inc., 2010.

Benrey, Ron. The Complete Idiot's Guide to Christian Mysteries. New York: Penguin Group, 2008.

Chadwick, Owen. A History of Christianity. New York: St. Martin's Press, 1995.

Collins, Michael, and Matthew A. Price. The Story of Christianity. New York: DK Publishing, Inc., 1999.

Geisler, Norman L., and William E. Nix. A General Introduction to the Bible. Chicago: Moody Press, 1986.

Hill, Jonathan. What Has Christianity Ever Done for Us? Downers Grove, IL: Intervarsity Press, 2005.

Zimmerman, Martha. Celebrating the Christian Year. Minneapolis: Bethany House Publishers, 1993.

On the Internet

Christian Apologetics and Research Ministry
  www.carm.org

Christianity Today

http://www.christianitytoday.com/ct/2013/
Christianity in View
www.christianityinview.com
The Christian Post
www.christianpost.com
Why Christmas?
www.whychristmas.com

Glossary

Advent (AD-vent)—From the Latin meaning "to come." The four weeks before Christmas during which Christians spiritually prepare for the coming of Christ.

Annunciation (uh-nun-see-AY-shun)—The announcement by the angel Gabriel to the Virgin Mary that she would conceive and become the mother of Jesus Christ.

apostle (uh-POSS-ul)—In the first century, the disciples chosen to travel and preach the Gospel message.

Ascension (uh-SEN-shun)—Christ's rising up to Heaven as witnessed by his apostles forty days after the Resurrection.

baptism (BAP-tizum)—Whether by full immersion or by the pouring or sprinkling of water, this rite symbolizes the believer's death to sin and rebirth to eternal life.

Bible (BY-bull)—The church's sacred text, divided into two parts—the Old Testament and the New Testament.

Christ (KRYST)—"The Anointed," a title of honor the Christians bestow on Jesus, indicating that he is Lord.

creed—From the Latin meaning "I believe." A summary of faith, such as the Apostles' Creed for Christians.

crucify (KROO-sih-fy)—To put to death by nailing or tying a person's hands and feet to a cross.

denomination (deh-nom-ih-NAY-shun)—A group of Christian congregations that share distinct teachings, rituals, and organization.

disciple (dih-SY-pull)—A pupil or follower of a specific teacher.

doctrine (DOK-trin)—The formal beliefs or tenets of faith as taught by a particular church.

Easter (EE-stur)—The celebration of Christ's resurrection from the dead.

eucharist (YOO-kuh-rist)—A sacrament that celebrates Christ's Last Supper through the partaking of bread and wine. It is also known as Holy Communion and the Lord's Supper.

excommunication (eks-kuh-myoo-nih-KAY-shun)—The act of banishing a person from the church and its activities.

Gospel (GAH-spull)—From the Greek meaning "good news." For Christians this is the message of salvation through Christ.

Incarnation (in-kar-NAY-shun)—The teaching that the second Person of the Trinity took on flesh and became human (Jesus).

indulgence (in-DUL-jents)—a paper given by an official of the Catholic church saying a person has been excused from a sin. Martin Luther opposed the sale of indulgences, saying forgiveness is a free gift of grace.

martyr (MAR-tur)—A person who dies for his faith.

messiah (muh-SY-uh)—In the Old Testament,, the promised deliverer of the Jewish nation.

nativity (nuh-TIH-vih-tee)—The birth of Jesus.

orthodox (ORTH-uh-doks)—From the Greek meaning "true teaching," the true or accepted doctrine of the church.

Pentateuch (PEN-tuh-tuke)—The first five books of the Old Testament, written by Moses.

Pope—The leader of the Roman Catholic Church.

Resurrection (rez-er-REK-shun)—Jesus's rising from the dead three days after his death and burial.

sacrament (SAK-ruh-mint)—A sacred act, such as baptism or communion, regarded as an outward and visible sign of divine grace.

trinity (TRIN-uh-tee)—The Christian teaching that the Godhead consists of three divine Persons—Father, Son, and Holy Spirit.

Yahweh (YAH-way)—From the Hebrew, meaning, "I am" or "He is," another name for God.

Ann Tatlock is a novelist and children's book author. Her works have received numerous awards, including the Silver Angel Award for Excellence in Media and the Midwest Book Award. She lives in the Blue Ridge Mountains of Western North Carolina with her husband and daughter. Find out more about Ann at http://anntatlock.com.